The
★ UNITED ★
STATES
PRESIDENTS

Bill
CLINTON

BreAnn Rumsch

Big Buddy Books
An Imprint of Abdo Publishing
abdopublishing.com

abdopublishing.com

Published by Abdo Publishing, a division of ABDO, PO Box 398166, Minneapolis, Minnesota 55439.
Copyright © 2017 by Abdo Consulting Group, Inc. International copyrights reserved in all countries. No part of this book may be reproduced in any form without written permission from the publisher. Big Buddy Books™ is a trademark and logo of Abdo Publishing.

Printed in the United States of America, North Mankato, Minnesota
062016
092016

THIS BOOK CONTAINS
RECYCLED MATERIALS

Design: Sarah DeYoung, Mighty Media, Inc.
Production: Mighty Media, Inc.
Editor: Paige Polinsky
Cover Photograph: Getty Images
Interior Photographs: AP Images (pp. 6, 7, 15, 17, 19, 21, 23, 27); Corbis (pp. 9, 11, 13);
    Getty Images (pp. 5, 7, 25, 29)

Cataloging-in-Publication Data

Names: Rumsch, BreAnn., author.
Title: Bill Clinton / by BreAnn Rumsch.
Description: Minneapolis, MN : Abdo Publishing, [2017] | Series: United States
    presidents | Includes bibliographical references and index.
Identifiers: LCCN 2015957279 | ISBN 9781680780895 (lib. bdg.) |
    ISBN 9781680775099 (ebook)
Subjects: LCSH: Clinton, Bill, 1946- --Juvenile literature. | Presidents--United
    States--Biography--Juvenile literature. | United States--Politics and
    government--1993-2001--Juvenile literature.
Classification: DDC 973.929/092 [B]--dc23
LC record available at http://lccn.loc.gov/2015957279

Contents

Bill Clinton

Bill Clinton was the forty-second president of the United States. As a young man, Clinton taught law. He later served as **attorney general** and state governor of Arkansas.

Clinton became president in 1993. He worked to improve the **economy**. Clinton also helped make peace in other nations.

President Clinton was reelected in 1997. Despite his **impeachment** in 1998, he continued to work hard for Americans. After his final term, Clinton remained active in community service.

Timeline

1946

On August 19, William Jefferson Clinton was born in Hope, Arkansas.

1979

Clinton became governor of Arkansas.

1973

Clinton **graduated** from Yale Law School in New Haven, Connecticut.

1993

On January 20, Clinton became the forty-second US president.

1998

The US House of Representatives **impeached** Clinton in December.

2002

Clinton started the Clinton Foundation.

1996

President Clinton was elected to a second term.

1999

On February 12, the US Senate found Clinton not guilty of lying under **oath**.

Early Years

William "Bill" Jefferson Blythe was born on August 19, 1946, in Hope, Arkansas. His parents were William and Virginia Blythe. William died before Bill was born. When Bill was two, Virginia moved to Louisiana.

Bill lived with his grandparents. Two years later, Virginia returned. She married Roger Clinton.

★ FAST FACTS ★

Born: August 19, 1946

Wife: Hillary Rodham (1947–)

Children: one

Political Party: Democrat

Age at Inauguration: 46

Years Served: 1993–2001

Vice President: Al Gore

Bill (*left*), his mother, and his brother, Roger

A Future Leader

Bill had a difficult home life. But he wanted to share his family's name. So, he chose to change his last name to Clinton.

In high school, Bill was very busy. He was involved in band and student government. In 1964, Bill **graduated** from high school.

Bill attended Georgetown University in Washington, DC. There, he studied **politics** and world issues. Bill graduated in 1968. Then, he attended Oxford University in England. He studied there for two years.

In 1963, Bill met President John F. Kennedy (*right*). The meeting led Bill to work in government.

Law and Marriage

In 1970, Clinton went to Yale Law School in New Haven, Connecticut. He also taught law at the University of New Haven. Clinton **graduated** from Yale in 1973.

That spring, Clinton became a **lawyer**. He began teaching law at the University of Arkansas. In 1974, Clinton ran for the US House of Representatives. He lost the race.

On October 11, 1975, Clinton married Hillary Rodham. Their daughter, Chelsea, was born in 1980.

Clinton met Hillary (*right*) at Yale. They worked on South Dakota senator George McGovern's presidential campaign together.

Governor Clinton

In 1976, Clinton became Arkansas **attorney general**. Three years later, he was elected state governor. Governor Clinton worked to improve schools and repair roads. To pay for these programs, he raised taxes. This upset voters.

Meanwhile, thousands of Cuban **refugees** came to Arkansas. Their care cost taxpayers a lot of money. In 1980, Clinton lost reelection. So, he returned to practicing law. Clinton joined a law firm in Little Rock, Arkansas.

Clinton served as Arkansas's attorney general for two years.

Return to Politics

Clinton ran for governor again in 1982. He won the election. Clinton went on to be reelected three more times. Governor Clinton supported laws to improve education. He improved the **economy** too. Clinton worked on laws that brought businesses to Arkansas.

In 1992, the **Democratic** Party chose Clinton to be president. The **Republicans** selected President George H.W. Bush. Voters hoped Clinton could improve the poor national economy. So, Clinton won the election!

Clinton chose Tennessee senator Al Gore (*left*) for his vice president. He and Gore were elected on November 3, 1992.

President Clinton

Clinton took office on January 20, 1993. Congress soon passed many laws he backed. One bill tightened gun control laws.

Soon, Clinton addressed America's health care system. He wanted to give all Americans health **insurance**. But Congress voted against it.

Clinton also worked on **NAFTA**. The agreement took effect in 1994. It greatly improved trade.

SUPREME COURT APPOINTMENTS

Ruth Bader Ginsburg: 1993

Stephen G. Breyer: 1994

In February 1993, Clinton signed the Family and Medical Leave Act. The act gives workers time off to care for a new baby or sick family member.

Clinton worked with other countries too. In 1993, he helped Israel and Palestine form a peace agreement. And in 1995, Clinton sent US troops to Bosnia. They helped keep peace there.

Meanwhile, the Clintons faced personal problems. They were charged with making illegal land deals. In 1996, Clinton's business partners were found guilty. But, the charges against the Clintons were dropped.

That same year, Clinton ran for reelection. The **Republican** Party selected Senator Bob Dole of Kansas. Clinton easily won the election. He began his second term on January 20, 1997.

Clinton encouraged peace talks between Israeli leader Yitzhak Rabin (*left*) and Palestinian leader Yasir Arafat (*right*).

Second Term

Clinton's second term involved much conflict. In 1998, **terrorists** based in Afghanistan attacked US **embassies** in Africa. Clinton ordered military attacks against the terrorists.

At this time, the **United Nations (UN)** feared Iraq was making dangerous weapons. Iraq would not let the UN inspect its factories. So, Clinton ordered attacks against Iraq.

★ DID YOU KNOW? ★

Clinton stays active by jogging and golfing. He also likes to do crossword puzzles.

PRESIDENT CLINTON'S CABINET

First Term
January 20, 1993–January 20, 1997

★ **STATE:** Warren M. Christopher
★ **TREASURY:** Lloyd Bentsen Jr.,
Robert E. Rubin (from January 10, 1995)
★ **ATTORNEY GENERAL:** Janet Reno
★ **INTERIOR:** Bruce Babbitt
★ **AGRICULTURE:** Mike Espy,
Dan Glickman (from March 30, 1995)
★ **COMMERCE:** Ronald H. Brown,
Mickey Kantor (from April 12, 1996)
★ **LABOR:** Robert B. Reich
★ **DEFENSE:** Les Aspin,
William J. Perry (from February 3, 1994)
★ **HEALTH AND HUMAN SERVICES:**
Donna E. Shalala
★ **HOUSING AND URBAN DEVELOPMENT:**
Henry G. Cisneros
★ **TRANSPORTATION:** Federico Peña
★ **ENERGY:** Hazel R. O'Leary
★ **EDUCATION:** Richard W. Riley
★ **VETERANS AFFAIRS:** Jesse Brown

Second Term
January 20, 1997–January 20, 2001

★ **STATE:** Madeleine Albright
★ **TREASURY:** Robert E. Rubin,
Lawrence H. Summers (from July 2, 1999)
★ **ATTORNEY GENERAL:** Janet Reno
★ **INTERIOR:** Bruce Babbitt
★ **AGRICULTURE:** Dan Glickman
★ **COMMERCE:** William M. Daley,
Norman Mineta (from July 21, 2000)
★ **LABOR:** Alexis M. Herman
★ **DEFENSE:** William Cohen
★ **HEALTH AND HUMAN SERVICES:**
Donna E. Shalala
★ **HOUSING AND URBAN DEVELOPMENT:**
Andrew M. Cuomo
★ **TRANSPORTATION:** Rodney Slater
★ **ENERGY:** Federico Peña,
Bill Richardson (from August 18, 1998)
★ **EDUCATION:** Richard W. Riley
★ **VETERANS AFFAIRS:** Togo D. West Jr.,
Hershel W. Gober (from July 25, 2000)

In 1999, the Clintons spoke to troops serving in Europe.

23

Back home, Clinton reduced government spending. The **economy** continued to grow. By 1998, many more people had homes and jobs.

Meanwhile, Clinton faced another personal problem. In 1994, a woman named Paula Jones had **sued** him. A judge threw out the case in April 1998. However, Jones **appealed** the decision. And, **lawyer** Kenneth Starr wanted to question Clinton further.

On August 17, 1998, Clinton appeared in court. Three months later, he paid Jones to drop the case. But his problems were not yet over.

Starr made sure Clinton's trial remained fair. He had also led Clinton's land deal investigation in 1996.

Impeachment

That September, Starr accused Clinton of lying under **oath**. So in December 1998, the House of Representatives **impeached** Clinton. Next, the US Senate held a trial. But on February 12, 1999, they found Clinton not guilty. So, he was allowed to remain president.

Clinton continued to work hard. In 2000, he improved trade with China and Vietnam. He also helped Vice President Gore run for president. However, Gore lost to Texas governor George W. Bush.

In 2000, Clinton helped his wife become a US senator. Hillary was elected by the people of New York.

Moving On

In January 2001, the Clintons left the White House. They moved to New York. The next year, Clinton started the Clinton Foundation. It works toward global health and social wellness.

In 2008, Hillary ran for president. Clinton supported her. But she later withdrew. On April 12, 2015, Hillary again entered the presidential race. Clinton often gave advice to her team.

While in office, Bill Clinton fought to improve social and **economic** problems. Today, he works to make the world a better place.

Clinton travels to parts of the world where the Clinton Foundation works.

Office of the President

Branches of Government

The US government has three branches. They are the executive, legislative, and judicial branches. Each branch has some power over the others. This is called a system of checks and balances.

★ Executive Branch

The executive branch enforces laws. It is made up of the president, the vice president, and the president's cabinet. The president represents the United States around the world. He or she also signs bills into law and leads the military.

★ Legislative Branch

The legislative branch makes laws, maintains the military, and regulates trade. It also has the power to declare war. This branch includes the Senate and the House of Representatives. Together, these two houses form Congress.

★ Judicial Branch

The judicial branch interprets laws. It is made up of district courts, courts of appeals, and the Supreme Court. District courts try cases. Sometimes people disagree with a trial's outcome. Then he or she may appeal. If a court of appeals supports the ruling, a person may appeal to the Supreme Court.

Qualifications for Office

To be president, a candidate must be at least 35 years old. The person must be a natural-born US citizen. He or she must also have lived in the United States for at least 14 years.

Electoral College

The US presidential election is an indirect election. Voters from each state choose electors. These electors represent their state in the Electoral College. Each elector has one electoral vote. Electors cast their vote for the candidate with the highest number of votes from people in their state. A candidate must receive the majority of Electoral College votes to win.

Term of Office

Each president may be elected to two four-year terms. The presidential election is held on the Tuesday after the first Monday in November. The president is sworn in on January 20 of the following year. At that time, he or she takes the oath of office.
It states:

> I do solemnly swear (or affirm) that I will faithfully execute the office of President of the United States, and will to the best of my ability, preserve, protect and defend the Constitution of the United States.

31

Line of Succession

The Presidential Succession Act of 1947 states who becomes president if the president cannot serve. The vice president is first in the line. Next are the Speaker of the House and the President Pro Tempore of the Senate. It may happen that none of these individuals is able to serve. Then the office falls to the president's cabinet members. They would take office in the order in which each department was created:

Secretary of State

Secretary of the Treasury

Secretary of Defense

Attorney General

Secretary of the Interior

Secretary of Agriculture

Secretary of Commerce

Secretary of Labor

Secretary of Health and Human Services

Secretary of Housing and Urban Development

Secretary of Transportation

Secretary of Energy

Secretary of Education

Secretary of Veterans Affairs

Secretary of Homeland Security

Benefits

★ While in office, the president receives a salary. It is $400,000 per year. He or she lives in the White House. The president also has 24-hour Secret Service protection.

★ The president may travel on a Boeing 747 jet. This special jet is called Air Force One. It can hold 70 passengers. It has kitchens, a dining room, sleeping areas, and more. Air Force One can fly halfway around the world before needing to refuel. It can even refuel in flight!

★ When the president travels by car, he or she uses Cadillac One. It is a Cadillac Deville that has been modified. The car has heavy armor and communications systems. The president may even take Cadillac One along when visiting other countries.

★ The president also travels on a helicopter. It is called Marine One. It may also be taken along when the president visits other countries.

★ Sometimes the president needs to get away with family and friends. Camp David is the official presidential retreat. It is located in Maryland. The US Navy maintains the retreat. The US Marine Corps keeps it secure. The camp offers swimming, tennis, golf, and hiking.

★ When the president leaves office, he or she receives lifetime Secret Service protection. He or she also receives a yearly pension of $203,700. The former president also receives money for office space, supplies, and staff.

PRESIDENTS AND THEIR TERMS

PRESIDENT	PARTY	TOOK OFFICE	LEFT OFFICE	TERMS SERVED	VICE PRESIDENT
George Washington	None	April 30, 1789	March 4, 1797	Two	John Adams
John Adams	Federalist	March 4, 1797	March 4, 1801	One	Thomas Jefferson
Thomas Jefferson	Democratic-Republican	March 4, 1801	March 4, 1809	Two	Aaron Burr, George Clinton
James Madison	Democratic-Republican	March 4, 1809	March 4, 1817	Two	George Clinton, Elbridge Gerry
James Monroe	Democratic-Republican	March 4, 1817	March 4, 1825	Two	Daniel D. Tompkins
John Quincy Adams	Democratic-Republican	March 4, 1825	March 4, 1829	One	John C. Calhoun
Andrew Jackson	Democrat	March 4, 1829	March 4, 1837	Two	John C. Calhoun, Martin Van Buren
Martin Van Buren	Democrat	March 4, 1837	March 4, 1841	One	Richard M. Johnson
William H. Harrison	Whig	March 4, 1841	April 4, 1841	Died During First Term	John Tyler
John Tyler	Whig	April 6, 1841	March 4, 1845	Completed Harrison's Term	Office Vacant
James K. Polk	Democrat	March 4, 1845	March 4, 1849	One	George M. Dallas
Zachary Taylor	Whig	March 5, 1849	July 9, 1850	Died During First Term	Millard Fillmore

PRESIDENT	PARTY	TOOK OFFICE	LEFT OFFICE	TERMS SERVED	VICE PRESIDENT
Millard Fillmore	Whig	July 10, 1850	March 4, 1853	Completed Taylor's Term	Office Vacant
Franklin Pierce	Democrat	March 4, 1853	March 4, 1857	One	William R.D. King
James Buchanan	Democrat	March 4, 1857	March 4, 1861	One	John C. Breckinridge
Abraham Lincoln	Republican	March 4, 1861	April 15, 1865	Served One Term, Died During Second Term	Hannibal Hamlin, Andrew Johnson
Andrew Johnson	Democrat	April 15, 1865	March 4, 1869	Completed Lincoln's Second Term	Office Vacant
Ulysses S. Grant	Republican	March 4, 1869	March 4, 1877	Two	Schuyler Colfax, Henry Wilson
Rutherford B. Hayes	Republican	March 3, 1877	March 4, 1881	One	William A. Wheeler
James A. Garfield	Republican	March 4, 1881	September 19, 1881	Died During First Term	Chester Arthur
Chester Arthur	Republican	September 20, 1881	March 4, 1885	Completed Garfield's Term	Office Vacant
Grover Cleveland	Democrat	March 4, 1885	March 4, 1889	One	Thomas A. Hendricks
Benjamin Harrison	Republican	March 4, 1889	March 4, 1893	One	Levi P. Morton
Grover Cleveland	Democrat	March 4, 1893	March 4, 1897	One	Adlai E. Stevenson
William McKinley	Republican	March 4, 1897	September 14, 1901	Served One Term, Died During Second Term	Garret A. Hobart, Theodore Roosevelt

PRESIDENT	PARTY	TOOK OFFICE	LEFT OFFICE	TERMS SERVED	VICE PRESIDENT
Theodore Roosevelt	Republican	September 14, 1901	March 4, 1909	Completed McKinley's Second Term, Served One Term	Office Vacant, Charles Fairbanks
William Taft	Republican	March 4, 1909	March 4, 1913	One	James S. Sherman
Woodrow Wilson	Democrat	March 4, 1913	March 4, 1921	Two	Thomas R. Marshall
Warren G. Harding	Republican	March 4, 1921	August 2, 1923	Died During First Term	Calvin Coolidge
Calvin Coolidge	Republican	August 3, 1923	March 4, 1929	Completed Harding's Term, Served One Term	Office Vacant, Charles Dawes
Herbert Hoover	Republican	March 4, 1929	March 4, 1933	One	Charles Curtis
Franklin D. Roosevelt	Democrat	March 4, 1933	April 12, 1945	Served Three Terms, Died During Fourth Term	John Nance Garner, Henry A. Wallace, Harry S. Truman
Harry S. Truman	Democrat	April 12, 1945	January 20, 1953	Completed Roosevelt's Fourth Term, Served One Term	Office Vacant, Alben Barkley
Dwight D. Eisenhower	Republican	January 20, 1953	January 20, 1961	Two	Richard Nixon
John F. Kennedy	Democrat	January 20, 1961	November 22, 1963	Died During First Term	Lyndon B. Johnson
Lyndon B. Johnson	Democrat	November 22, 1963	January 20, 1969	Completed Kennedy's Term, Served One Term	Office Vacant, Hubert H. Humphrey
Richard Nixon	Republican	January 20, 1969	August 9, 1974	Completed First Term, Resigned During Second Term	Spiro T. Agnew, Gerald Ford

PRESIDENT	PARTY	TOOK OFFICE	LEFT OFFICE	TERMS SERVED	VICE PRESIDENT
Gerald Ford	Republican	August 9, 1974	January 20, 1977	Completed Nixon's Second Term	Nelson A. Rockefeller
Jimmy Carter	Democrat	January 20, 1977	January 20, 1981	One	Walter Mondale
Ronald Reagan	Republican	January 20, 1981	January 20, 1989	Two	George H.W. Bush
George H.W. Bush	Republican	January 20, 1989	January 20, 1993	One	Dan Quayle
Bill Clinton	Democrat	January 20, 1993	January 20, 2001	Two	Al Gore
George W. Bush	Republican	January 20, 2001	January 20, 2009	Two	Dick Cheney
Barack Obama	Democrat	January 20, 2009	January 20, 2017	Two	Joe Biden

"There is nothing wrong with America that cannot be cured by what is right with America." Bill Clinton

★ WRITE TO THE PRESIDENT ★

You may write to the president at:
The White House
1600 Pennsylvania Avenue NW
Washington, DC 20500

You may e-mail the president at:
comments@whitehouse.gov

37

Glossary

appeal—to ask a higher court to review a decision of a lower court.

attorney general—the chief lawyer of a country or state who represents the government in legal matters.

Democratic—relating to the Democratic political party. Democrats believe in social change and strong government.

economy—the way that a country produces, sells, and buys goods and services. The study of this is called economics.

embassy—the residence and offices of an ambassador in a foreign country.

graduate (GRA-juh-wayt)—to complete a level of schooling.

impeach—to charge someone for doing wrong while serving in a public office.

insurance—a contract that promises to guard people against a loss of money if something happens to them or their property.

lawyer (LAW-yuhr)—a person who gives people advice on laws or represents them in court.

NAFTA—North American Free Trade Agreement. An agreement signed by Canada, Mexico, and the United States to increase trade.

oath—a formal promise or statement.

politics—the art or science of government. Something referring to politics is political. A person who is active in politics is a politician.

refugee—someone who leaves their home in search of a safe place.

Republican—a member of the Republican political party.

sue—to bring legal action against a person or an organization.

terrorist—a person who uses violence to scare or control people or governments.

United Nations (UN)—a group of nations formed in 1945. Its goals are peace, human rights, security, and social and economic development.

★ WEBSITES ★

To learn more about the US Presidents, visit **booklinks.abdopublishing.com**. These links are routinely monitored and updated to provide the most current information available.

Index